Law and Crime

LEVEL 6
/i_e/
/igh/

Teaching Tips

Orange Level 6
This book focuses on the phonemes /i_e/igh/.

Before Reading
- Discuss the title. Ask readers what they think the book will be about. Have them briefly explain why.
- Ask readers to name the missing letter for each word on page 3. What do they notice about the "i" sound in these words? Is the "i" a long or short vowel in each?

Read the Book
- Encourage readers to break down unfamiliar words into units of sound. Then, ask them to string the sounds together to create the words.
- Urge readers to point out when the focused phonics phonemes appear in the text.

After Reading
- Encourage children to reread the book independently or with a friend.
- Ask readers to name other words with /i_e/ or /igh/ phonemes. On a separate sheet of paper, have them write the words out.

© 2024 Booklife Publishing
This edition is published by arrangement with Booklife Publishing.

North American adaptations © 2024 Jump!
5345 Penn Avenue South
Minneapolis, MN 55419
www.jumplibrary.com

Decodables by Jump! are published by Jump! Library.
All rights reserved. No part of this book may be reproduced in any form without written permission from the publisher.

Library of Congress Cataloging-in-Publication Data is available at www.loc.gov or upon request from the publisher.

ISBN: 979-8-88996-861-0 (hardcover)
ISBN: 979-8-88996-862-7 (paperback)
ISBN: 979-8-88996-863-4 (ebook)

Photo Credits
Images are courtesy of Shutterstock.com. With thanks to Getty Images, Thinkstock Photo and iStockphoto. Cover – theprint. 2–3 – MossStudio, Creatus, Nature Design, New Africa. 4–5 – kali9, Powerofflowers. 6–7 – Lucky Business, Mike_shots. 8–9 – Larisa Rudenko, Vitalii Stock. 10–11 – Brian Minkoff, Julian Popov. 12–13 – JaneHYork, LightField Studios. 14–15 – Simon Vayro, vystekimages. 16 – Shutterstock.

Can you fill in the gaps?

bi_e

pi_e

vi_e

sli_e

All people have to obey the law. Laws tell people what they can and cannot do. We say that a person has committed a crime when they do something that is against the law.

Crime can hurt the people who do it. It can hurt the people around them too. We have laws to protect people.

Stealing is a crime. It is against the law to take things from a store without paying for them.

Fighting is a crime unless you are in a fighting sport, such as boxing. People who fight for sport still have to obey the laws to keep people from getting hurt.

Boxer

To drive, you must pass a test about traffic laws. When you finish, you will get a card that says you are allowed to drive.

Trespassing is when you go somewhere you are not allowed to be. Do not trespass on a site if a person tells you that you cannot be there.

People who commit crimes are criminals. If they hide from the law, people will come looking for them so they can arrest them.

A criminal will have a hard time getting out of handcuffs. They are locked on tight so that the suspect cannot slide out.

Handcuffs

For lesser crimes, criminals might get a fine. For bigger crimes, they may have to go to jail for a long time.

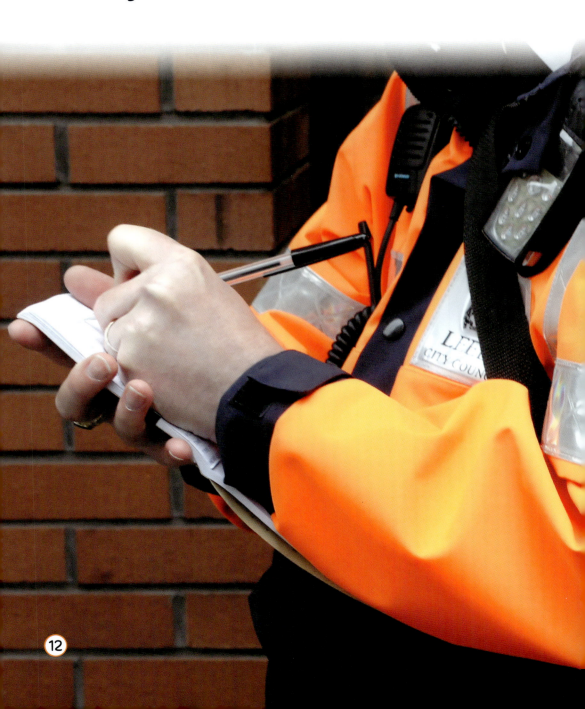

Some criminals might spend a few years in jail. Some might end up spending the rest of their lives there. They can never get out.

What can you do if you see a crime? You can call nine one one to get help.

Talk to an adult. Practice what you will do if you need to call nine one one.

Can you name the missing letters for each word?

5   f_v_

n___t

l___t